Presented to

_____

From

_____

Date

_____

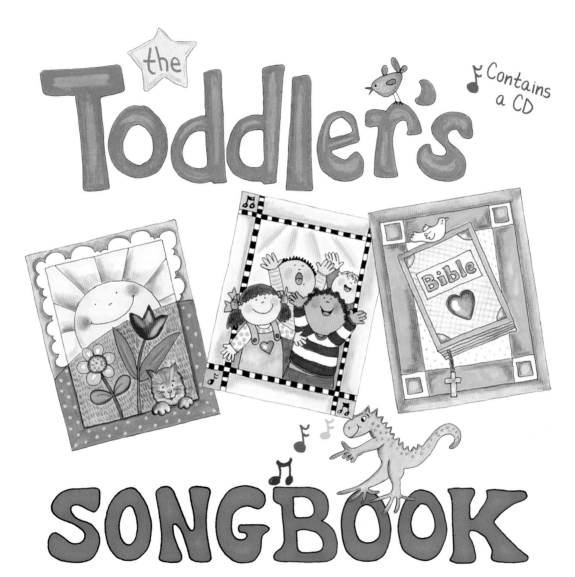

the Toddler's

Contains a CD

Bible

SONGBOOK

Ellen Banks Elwell & Illustrations by Caron Turk

The Toddler's Songbook

Copyright © 2009 Educational Publishing Concepts, Inc.

Published by Crossway Books
           a publishing ministry of Good News Publishers
           1300 Crescent Street
           Wheaton, Illinois 60187

Cover design and illustration: Caron Turk
First printing 2009
Printed in Singapore

Music Credits for CD

Executive Producer: Ellen Banks Elwell

Producer/Arranger: Larry Shackley

Music Director: Ellen Banks Elwell

Adult Vocal Soloist: Gail Pflederer

Youth Vocals: Lisa Couture, Nathan Elwell, Jaimee Harbeck, Jeff Harbeck, Julee Harbeck, Kim Huizingh, Beth Liebenow, Sarah Meyer, Ashley Petti, Josh Reynolds, Lucy Sullivan

Violin: Gail Salvatori

Cello: Kathy Beers Cathey

French Horn: Steve Pierson

Piano/Synthesizer: Larry Shackley

Hardback ISBN: 978-1-4335-0595-9
PDF ISBN: 978-1-4335-0596-6
Mobipocket ISBN: 978-1-4335-0597-3

Library of Congress Cataloging-in-Publication Data
The toddler's songbook / [compiled by] Ellen Banks Elwell & illustrations by Caron Turk.

    p. cm.

  Without music.

  Summary: "Seventeen familiar songs, each accompanied by a brief narrative"—Provided by publisher.

  ISBN 978-1-4335-0595-9 (hc)—ISBN 978-1-4335-0596-6 (PDF)—ISBN 978-1-4335-0597-3 (Mobipocket)
  1. Children's songs—Texts. I. Elwell, Ellen Banks, 1952– II. Turk, Caron, ill. III. Title.

  ML54.6.T73 2009

  782.42083'3—dc22

                                2009000525

IMG		15		14		13		12		11		10		09
9	8		7		6		5		4		3		2		1

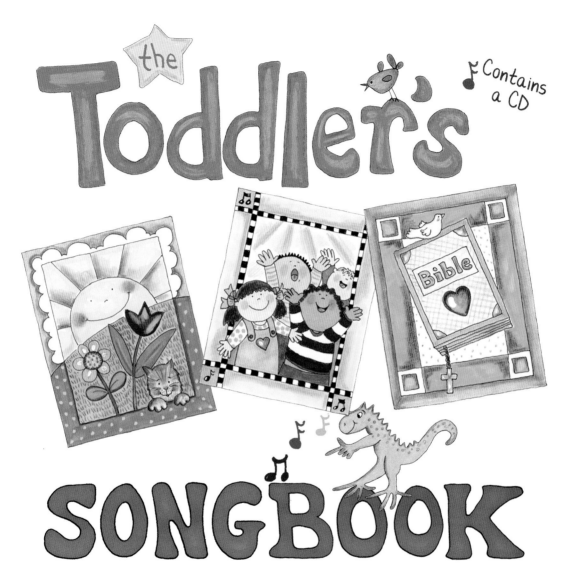

the
Toddler's

Contains a CD

SONGBOOK

Ellen Banks Elwell & Illustrations by Caron Turk

Crossway Books
Wheaton, Illinois

Contents

Rise and Shine

Open up your sleepy eyes.
It's time to rise and shine!

Throw back your blanket.
It's time to rise and shine!

Say hello to kitty.
It's time to rise and shine!

Thank you, God, for morning.
It's time to rise and shine!

Rise and shine and give God the glory, glory.
Rise and shine and give God the glory, glory.
Rise and shine and [clap] give God the glory, glory.
Children of the Lord.

13

Praise Him, Praise Him

Thank you, God, for loving all the children.
You love the children who like to be quiet.
You love the children who like to make noise.
You love the children with black or brown hair.
You love the children with blond or red hair.
Thank you, God, for loving all the children!

Praise him, praise him, all ye little children
God is love, God is love.
Praise him, praise him, all ye little children.
God is love, God is love.

Verse 2: Thank him, thank him. . . .

Verse 3: Serve him, serve him. . . .

Jesus Loves Me

Jesus loves me, I know.
How do I know?
God wrote it in the Bible.
That's how I know!

Jesus died for me, I know.
How do I know?
God wrote it in the Bible.
That's how I know!

Jesus cares for me, I know.
How do I know?
God wrote it in the Bible.
That's how I know!

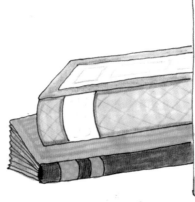

Jesus loves me, this I know,
For the Bible tells me so.
Little ones to him belong.
They are weak, but he is strong.
Yes, Jesus loves me.
Yes, Jesus loves me.
Yes, Jesus loves me.
The Bible tells me so.

17

If You're Happy

Sometimes we're happy.
Sometimes we're sad.
God knows when we're happy,
　　and he knows when we're sad.
Are you happy? Clap your hands!
Are you happy? Stomp your feet!
Are you happy? Say amen!
Thank you, God! You see us all the time.

If you're happy and you know it, clap your hands.
If you're happy and you know it, clap your hands.
If you're happy and you know it, and you really want to show it,
If you're happy and you know it, clap your hands.

Verse 2: If you're happy and you know it, stomp your feet. . . .

Verse 3: If you're happy and you know it, say amen! . . .

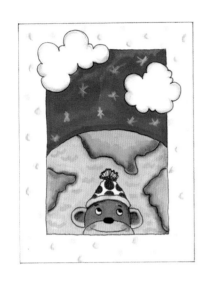

He's Got the Whole World in His Hands

God takes care of the whole wide world.
He takes care of the monkeys in the tree.
He takes care of the wind and the rain.
God takes care of you and me!

20

He's got the whole world in his hands,
He's got the whole world in his hands,
He's got the whole world in his hands,
He's got the whole world in his hands.

Verse 2: He's got the wind and the rain…

Verse 3: He's got the little bitty baby…

Verse 4: He's got you and me, brother…

Verse 5: Repeat verse 1

Mozart's Lullaby

Do you ever sleep in a tree?
No, but birds do. One, two, three.
Sleep on a hill? Do you do that?
No, but lambs do. One has a hat!
Sleepy animals. Sleepy me.
God made sleep.
God made me!

22

Sleep, baby, sleep, and good night,
All the birds are asleep out of sight.
Quiet the lambs on the hill.
Even the bumblebee's still.
Only the man in the moon
Still is a-nodding, but soon
Over him slumber will creep.
Sleep, baby, sleep, go to sleep.
Good night, good night.

23

Hallelujah, Praise the Lord

Hallelujah is a very big word.
Hallelujah means praise the Lord!
Thank you, God, for who you are.
Thank you, God, for all you do.
Hallelujah! God loves the world!
Hallelujah! God loves me!

Hallelu, hallelu, hallelu, hallelujah,
Praise ye the Lord.
Hallelu, hallelu, hallelu, hallelujah,
Praise ye the Lord.
Praise ye the Lord, hallelujah.
Praise ye the Lord, hallelujah.
Praise ye the Lord, hallelujah.
Praise ye the Lord.

Old MacDonald

God made the animals. Do you know their sounds?
God made the chicks. Cluck-cluck, chicks!
God made the ducks. Quack-quack, ducks!
God made the pigs. Oink-oink, pigs!
God made the cows. Moo-moo, cows!
God made the animals. Can you say their sounds?

Old MacDonald had a farm, E-I-E-I-O.
And on this farm he had some chicks, E-I-E-I-O.
With a chick-chick here, and a chick-chick there,
Here a chick, there a chick, everywhere a chick-chick,
Old MacDonald had a farm, E-I-E-I-O.

Verse 2: Ducks; quack-quack

Verse 3: Pigs; oink-oink

Verse 4: Cows; moo-moo

27

God Is So Good

God is good—all the time.
Only God is good all the time.
God loves me. All the time.
God loves everyone all the time.
God hears me. All the time.
Thank you, God—I can pray anytime!

JANUARY
FEBRUARY
MARCH
APRIL
MAY
JUNE
JULY
AUGUST
SEPTEMBER
OCTOBER
NOVEMBER
DECEMBER

28

God is so good, God is so good.
God is so good. He's so good to me.

Verse 2: God loves me so. . . .

Verse 3: God answers prayer. . . .

Verse 3: God is so good. . . .

Who Did?

Who swallowed Jonah? Was it a black horse?
No, not a horse that swallowed Jonah, of course!
Who swallowed Jonah? Was it a big fish?
Yes! That's who it was! Swish, swish, swish!
Even though Jonah hadn't chosen to obey,
God used a fish to help Jonah find his way.

Who did, who did, who did, who did,
Who did swallow Jo-jo-jo-jo?
Who did, who did, who did, who did,
Who did swallow Jo-jo-jo-jo?
Who did, who did, who did, who did,
Who did swallow Jo-jo-jo-jo?
Who did swallow Jonah? Who did swallow Jonah?
Who did swallow Jonah down?

Verse 2: Big fish, big fish, big fish, big fish,
Big fish swallowed Jo-jo-jo-jo. . . .
Big fish swallowed Jonah down.

Zacchaeus

Zacchaeus was a wee little man,
Way too little for him to see Jesus.
Zacchaeus had a great big idea.
Up in a tree, he could see Jesus!
Jesus saw Zacchaeus in the tree.
Jesus said, "Come be with me!"

Zacchaeus was a wee little man, a wee little man was he.
He climbed up in a sycamore tree, for the Lord he wanted to see.
And as the Savior passed that way, he looked up in the tree.
And he said, "Zacchaeus, you come down!"
For I'm going to your house today,
For I'm going to your house today.

Mary Had a Baby

Mary saw an angel, who came from God.
"You will have a baby," the angel said.
Mary had a baby, and laid him in a manger.
She wrapped her baby in soft, soft clothes.
Mary named him Jesus. Shepherds came to visit.
God has done great things, Mary thought.

Mary had a baby, Mary had a baby.
O Mary had a baby, Mary had a baby,
Mary had a baby, O Lord.

Verse 2: Where did she lay him? . . .

Verse 3: Laid him in a manger. . . .

Verse 4: What did she name him? . . .

Verse 5: Mary named him Jesus. . . .

Verse 6: Ooh. . . .

Twinkle, Twinkle, Little Star

Have you seen the stars at night?
Shining in the sky so bright.
How many stars are in the sky?
Only God knows. My, oh, my!
Do you know God made each one?
Finding stars is lots of fun.

Twinkle, twinkle, little star,
How I wonder what you are.
Up above the world so high,
Like a diamond in the sky.
Twinkle, twinkle, little star,
How I wonder what you are.

Verse 2: When the blazing sun is gone,
When he nothing shines upon;
Then you show your little light,
Twinkle, twinkle, all the night.
Twinkle, twinkle, little star,
How I wonder what you are.

Oh, Be Careful

Oh, be careful, little eyes.
God wants you to see good things.
Oh, be careful, little ears.
God wants you to hear good things.
Oh, be careful, little mouth.
God wants you to say good things.
Oh, be careful, little hands.
God wants you to do good things.
Oh, be careful, little friend.
God wants you to choose good things.

Oh, be careful little eyes what you see.
Oh, be careful little eyes what you see.
For the Father up above is looking down in love.
Oh, be careful little eyes what you see.

Verse 2: Oh, be careful little ears what you hear. . . .

Verse 3: Oh, be careful little mind what you think. . . .

Verse 4: Oh, be careful little hands what you do. . . .

Verse 5: Oh, be careful little feet where you go. . . .

Jesus loves me this I know

Little David, Play on Your Harp

David loved God very much.
David liked to sing to God.
Sometimes, David cared for sheep.
Sometimes, David played his harp.
Can you point to David's sheep?
Can you point to David's harp?

Little David, play on your harp, hallelu, hallelu.
Little David play on your harp, hallelu.
Little David, play on your harp, hallelu, hallelu.
Little David play on your harp, hallelu.
Little David was a shepherd boy.
He killed Goliath and shouted for joy.
Little David, play on your harp, hallelu, hallelu.
Little David play on your harp, hallelu.
Little David, play on your harp, hallelu, hallelu.
Little David, play on your harp, hallelu.

Oh, How Lovely Is the Evening

Evening time. Yummy supper.
Evening time. Want to read?
Evening time. Big, big yawn.
Evening time. Let's pray.
Evening time. Close your eyes.
Evening time. God never sleeps!

♪ Oh, how lovely is the evening, is the evening,
When the bells are sweetly ringing, sweetly ringing,
Ding, dong, ding, dong, ding, dong.

43

All through the Night

While you sleep, you're not alone,
Not alone inside your home.
Someone watches over you,
Watches o'er your family, too.
God sees you throughout the night,
All the way to morning light.

44

Sleep, my child, and peace attend thee,
All through the night.
Guardian angels God will send thee,
All through the night.
Soft the drowsy hours are creeping,
Hill and dale in slumber sleeping,
I, my loving vigil keeping,
All through the night.

45